THIS LITTLE
TRAILBLAZER
A GIRL POWER PRIMER

ISBN 978-1-338-28179-8

12 11 10 9 8 7 6 5 4 3 2 1   18 19 20 21 22 23

Printed in the U.S.A.   40

First Scholastic printing, January 2018

Designed by Laura Roode

THIS LITTLE
TRAILBLAZER
A GIRL POWER PRIMER

JOAN HOLUB

DANIEL ROODE

SCHOLASTIC INC.

Paving the way
to a future that's bright.

Helping the world with their skills, smarts, and might.

Little trailblazers cause great big changes.

ADA LOVELACE

This little trailblazer helped think of a way to do math with machines, called computers today!

Ada Lovelace wrote one of the first computer programs. The US government later named a computer language "Ada" in her honor.

FLORENCE
NIGHTINGALE

This little trailblazer
had the courage and skill
to organize hospitals
and care for the ill.

Florence Nightingale began the first professional school for nurses. She was nicknamed the Lady with the Lamp.

COCO CHANEL

This little trailblazer became a millionaire by designing simpler clothes for women to wear.

Coco Chanel disliked the tight dresses of the early 1900s. She created comfortable styles that women still love today.

ROSA PARKS

This little trailblazer
caused a big fuss
by not giving up
her seat on the bus.

Rosa Parks's bravery helped change an unfair rule that African Americans could not sit by Caucasians on the bus.

MARIA
TALLCHIEF

This little trailblazer
practiced hard at the barre.
In the *Firebird* ballet,
she soared like a star!

Maria Tallchief was the first prima ballerina of the New York City Ballet, and the first world-famous Native American ballerina.

WILMA RUDOLPH

This little trailblazer
could run, jump, and throw.
When she hit the track,
crowds cheered, "Go, Wilma, go!"

Wilma Rudolph wore a leg brace as a girl.
Yet she became the first American woman to win
three Olympic gold medals in track and field!

SONIA SOTOMAYOR

This little trailblazer can settle a fight about whether a law is wrong or is right.

Sonia Sotomayor is the first Latina judge and third woman to serve on the Supreme Court of the United States.

RUBY BRIDGES

This little trailblazer marched to first grade and changed every school with each step she made.

Ruby Bridges was the first African American child at her school and helped change things so kids of all colors now learn together.

MAYA LIN

This little trailblazer designed a V-shaped wall carved with heroes' names that's beloved by all.

Maya Lin is the architect and sculptor who created the popular Vietnam Veterans Memorial in Washington DC.

MALALA
YOUSAFZAI

This little trailblazer
helps girls everywhere
to be treated in ways
that are kind and fair.

Malala Yousafzai wants all children to be free to go to school.
She is the youngest person to win the Nobel Peace Prize.

Computers, lawmaking, designing, ballet—

JOAN OF ARC

A teenage girl, who led the French army to fight England in the 1400s.

ELIZABETH CADY STANTON

First woman to run for Congress. Co-organizer of the first US Women's Rights Convention.

HARRIET TUBMAN

A former slave, who led other slaves to freedom on the Underground Railroad.

ELIZABETH BLACKWELL

This doctor was the first woman in the US to earn a medical degree.

JULIETTE GORDON LOW

She began the first Girl Scout troop in the US to teach girls leadership skills.

NELLIE BLY

One of the first undercover news reporters she wrote about poor people's problems.

how will you change the world someday?

BESSIE COLEMAN

The first African American woman
to get a pilot's license to fly airplanes.

FRIDA KAHLO

One of Mexico's great artists, she is
famous for painting pictures of herself.

LUCILLE BALL

A superstar actress, who was the
first woman to run a major TV studio.

ELLA FITZGERALD

This jazz singer was the first African
American woman to win a Grammy Award.

INDIRA GANDHI

The first female
prime minister of India.

HILLARY CLINTON

First woman to run for president
of the United States with a major
political party.

YOU!